let's cook

potatoes

Jenny
Stacey

p

Contents

Leek, Potato & Bacon Soup

Leek and potato soup is a classic recipe. Here the soup is enhanced with smoked bacon pieces and enriched with double (heavy) cream for a little luxury.

Serves 4

INGREDIENTS

25 g/1 oz/2 tbsp butter
175 g/6 oz potatoes, diced
4 leeks, shredded
2 garlic cloves, crushed
100 g/3½ oz smoked bacon, diced

900 ml/1½ pints/3¾ cups vegetable stock
225 ml/8 fl oz/1 cup double (heavy) cream
2 tbsp chopped fresh parsley
salt and pepper

TO GARNISH:
vegetable oil
1 leek, shredded

1 Melt the butter in a large saucepan and add the diced potatoes, shredded leeks, garlic and diced bacon. Sauté gently for 5 minutes, stirring constantly.

2 Add the vegetable stock and bring to the boil. Reduce the heat, cover the saucepan and simmer for 20 minutes until the potatoes are cooked. Stir in the double (heavy) cream.

3 Meanwhile, make the garnish. Half-fill a pan with oil and heat to 180°C-190°C/350°F-375°F or until a cube of bread browns in 30 seconds. Add the shredded leek and deep-fry for 1 minute until browned and crisp, taking care as the leek contains water. Drain the leek thoroughly on paper towels and reserve.

4 Reserve a few pieces of potato, leek and bacon and set aside. Put the rest of the soup in a food processor or blender in batches and process each batch for 30 seconds. Return the puréed soup to a clean saucepan and heat through.

5 Stir in the reserved vegetables, bacon and parsley and season to taste. Pour into warmed bowls and garnish with the fried leeks.

VARIATION

For a lighter soup, omit the cream and stir yogurt or crème fraîche into the soup at the end of the cooking time.

Potato & Italian Sausage Salad

Sliced Italian sausage blends well with the other Mediterranean flavours of sun-dried tomato and basil in this salad. All of the flavours are relatively strong and therefore do not overpower each other.

Serves 4

INGREDIENTS

450 g/1 lb waxy potatoes
1 raddichio or lollo rosso lettuce
1 green (bell) pepper, sliced
175 g/6 oz Italian sausage, sliced
1 red onion, halved and sliced

125 g/4¹/₂ oz sun-dried tomatoes, sliced
2 tbsp shredded fresh basil

DRESSING:
1 tbsp balsamic vinegar
1 tsp tomato purée (paste)
2 tbsp olive oil
salt and pepper

1 Cook the potatoes in a saucepan of boiling water for 20 minutes or until cooked through. Drain and leave to cool.

2 Line a large serving platter with the radicchio or lollo rosso lettuce leaves.

3 Slice the cooled potatoes and arrange them in layers on the lettuce-lined serving platter together with the sliced green (bell) pepper, sliced Italian sausage, red onion, sun-dried tomatoes and shredded fresh basil.

4 In a small bowl, whisk the balsamic vinegar, tomato purée (paste) and olive oil together and season to taste with salt and pepper. Pour the dressing over the potato salad and serve immediately.

COOK'S TIP

You can use either packets of sun-dried tomatoes or jars of sun-dried tomatoes in oil. If using tomatoes packed in oil, simply rinse the oil from the tomatoes and pat them dry on paper towels before using.

VARIATION

Any sliced Italian sausage or salami can be used in this salad. Italy is home of the salami and there are numerous varieties to choose from – those from the south tend to be more highly spiced than those from the north of the country.

Potato & Tuna Salad

This colourful dish is a variation of the classic Salade Niçoise. Packed with tuna and vegetables, it is both filling and delicious.

Serves 4

INGREDIENTS

450 g/1 lb new potatoes, scrubbed and quartered
1 green (bell) pepper, sliced
50 g/1³/4 oz canned sweetcorn, drained
1 red onion, sliced

300 g/10¹/2 oz canned tuna in brine, drained and flaked
2 tbsp chopped stoned (pitted) black olives
salt and pepper
lime wedges, to garnish

DRESSING:
2 tbsp mayonnaise
2 tbsp soured cream
1 tbsp lime juice
2 garlic cloves, crushed
finely grated rind of 1 lime

1 Cook the potatoes in a saucepan of boiling water for 15 minutes until tender. Drain and leave to cool in a mixing bowl.

2 Gently stir in the sliced green (bell) pepper, sweetcorn and sliced red onion.

3 Spoon the potato mixture into a large serving bowl and arrange the flaked tuna and chopped black olives over the top. Season the salad generously with salt and pepper.

4 To make the dressing, mix together the mayonnaise, soured cream, lime juice, garlic and lime rind in a bowl.

5 Spoon the dressing over the tuna and olives, garnish with lime wedges and serve.

COOK'S TIP

Served with a crisp white wine, this salad makes the perfect light lunch for summer or winter.

VARIATION

Green beans and hard-boiled (hard-cooked) egg slices can be added to the salad for a more traditional Salade Niçoise.

Potato & Meatballs in Spicy Sauce

These meatballs are delicious served with warm crusty bread to 'mop up' the sauce. For a main meal, make half as much mixture again, rolling the balls into larger rounds; serve with rice and vegetables.

Serves 4

INGREDIENTS

225 g/8 oz floury (mealy) potatoes, diced
225 g/8 oz minced beef or lamb
1 onion, finely chopped
1 tbsp chopped fresh coriander (cilantro)
1 celery stick, finely chopped
2 garlic cloves, crushed

25 g/1 oz/2 tbsp butter
1 tbsp vegetable oil
salt and pepper
chopped fresh coriander (cilantro), to garnish

SAUCE:
1 tbsp vegetable oil

1 onion, finely chopped
2 tsp soft brown sugar
400 g/14 oz can chopped tomatoes
1 green chilli, chopped
1 tsp paprika
150 ml/^{1}/4 pint/^{2}/3 cup vegetable stock
2 tsp cornflour (cornstarch)

1 Cook the diced potatoes in a saucepan of boiling water for 25 minutes until cooked through. Drain well and transfer to a large mixing bowl. Mash until smooth.

2 Add the minced beef or lamb, onion, coriander (cilantro), celery and garlic and mix well.

3 Bring the mixture together with your hands and roll it into 20 small balls.

4 To make the sauce, heat the oil in a pan and sauté the onion for 5 minutes. Add the remaining sauce ingredients and bring to the boil, stirring. Lower the heat and simmer for 20 minutes.

5 Meanwhile, heat the butter and oil for the potato and meat balls in a frying pan (skillet). Add the balls in batches and cook for 10-15 minutes until browned, turning frequently. Keep warm whilst cooking the remainder. Serve the potato and meatballs in a warm shallow ovenproof dish with the sauce poured around them and garnished with coriander (cilantro).

COOK'S TIP

Make the potato and meatballs in advance and chill or freeze them for later use. Make sure you defrost them thoroughly before cooking.

Potato, Cheese & Onion Rosti

These grated potato cakes are also known as straw cakes, as they resemble a straw mat! Serve them with a tomato sauce or salad for a light supper dish.

Serves 4

INGREDIENTS

900 g/2 lb Maris Piper potatoes
1 onion, grated
50 g/2 oz Gruyère cheese, grated
2 tbsp chopped fresh parsley

1 tbsp olive oil
25 g/1 oz/2 tbsp butter
salt and pepper

TO GARNISH:
shredded spring onion (scallion)
1 small tomato, quartered

1 Parboil the potatoes in a pan of boiling water for 10 minutes and leave to cool. Peel the potatoes and grate with a coarse grater. Place the grated potatoes in a large mixing bowl.

2 Stir in the onion, cheese and parsley. Season well with salt and pepper. Divide the potato mixture into 4 portions of equal size and form them into cakes.

3 Heat half of the olive oil and butter in a frying pan (skillet) and cook 2 of the potato cakes over a high heat for 1 minute, then reduce the heat and cook for 5 minutes until they are golden underneath. Turn them over and cook for a further 5 minutes.

4 Repeat with the other half of the oil and butter to cook the remaining 2 cakes. Transfer to serving plates, garnish and serve.

COOK'S TIP

The potato cakes should be flattened as much as possible during cooking, otherwise the outside will be cooked before the centre.

VARIATION

To make these rosti into a more substantial meal, add chopped cooked bacon or ham to the potato mixture.

Potato Croquettes with Ham & Cheese

This is a classic potato dish which may be served plain as an accompaniment, or with added ingredients, such as other cooked vegetables or salami, and a cheese sauce as a snack.

Serves 4

INGREDIENTS

450 g/1 lb floury (mealy) potatoes, diced
300 ml/$\frac{1}{2}$ pint/1$\frac{1}{2}$ cups milk
25 g/1 oz/2 tbsp butter
4 spring onions (scallions), chopped
75 g/2$\frac{3}{4}$ oz Cheddar cheese
50 g/1$\frac{3}{4}$ oz smoked ham, chopped
1 celery stick, diced
1 egg, beaten

50 g/1$\frac{3}{4}$ oz/$\frac{1}{2}$ cup plain (all-purpose) flour
oil, for deep frying
salt and pepper

COATING:
2 eggs, beaten
125 g/4$\frac{1}{2}$ oz fresh wholemeal (whole wheat) breadcrumbs

SAUCE:
25 g/1 oz/2 tbsp butter
25 g/1 oz/ $\frac{1}{4}$ cup plain (all-purpose) flour
150 ml/$\frac{1}{4}$ pint/$\frac{2}{3}$ cup milk
150 ml/$\frac{1}{4}$ pint/$\frac{2}{3}$ cup vegetable stock
75 g/2$\frac{3}{4}$ oz Cheddar cheese, grated
1 tsp Dijon mustard
1 tbsp chopped coriander (cilantro)

1 Place the potatoes in a pan with the milk and bring to the boil. Reduce to a simmer until the liquid has been absorbed and the potatoes are cooked.

2 Add the butter and mash the potatoes. Stir in the spring onions (scallions), cheese, ham, celery, egg and flour. Season and leave to cool.

3 To make the coating, whisk the eggs in a bowl. Put the breadcrumbs in a separate bowl.

4 Shape the potato mixture into 8 balls. First dip them in the egg, then in the breadcrumbs.

5 To make the sauce, melt the butter in a small pan. Add the flour and cook for 1 minute.

Remove from the heat and stir in the milk, stock, cheese, mustard and herbs. Bring to the boil, stirring until thickened. Reduce the heat and keep warm.

6 In a deep fat fryer, heat the oil to 180°C-190°C/350°F-375°F and fry the croquettes for 5 minutes until golden. Drain well and serve with the sauce.

Hash Browns with Tomato Sauce

Hash Browns are a popular American recipe of fried potato squares, often served as brunch.
This recipe includes extra vegetables for a more substantial snack.

Serves 4

INGREDIENTS

450 g/1 lb waxy potatoes
1 carrot, diced
1 celery stick, diced
50 g/2 oz button mushrooms, diced
1 onion, diced
2 garlic cloves, crushed
25 g/1 oz frozen peas, thawed
50 g/2 oz Parmesan cheese, grated

4 tbsp vegetable oil
25 g/1 oz/2 tbsp butter
salt and pepper

SAUCE:
300 ml/^{1}/$_2$ pint/1^1/$_4$ cups passata
2 tbsp chopped fresh coriander
1 tbsp Worcestershire sauce

^{1}/$_2$ tsp chilli powder
2 tsp brown sugar
2 tsp American mustard
85 ml/3 fl oz/^{1}/$_3$ cup vegetable stock

1 Cook the potatoes in a saucepan of boiling water for 10 minutes. Drain and leave to cool. Meanwhile, cook the carrot in boiling water for 5 minutes.

2 When cool, grate the potato with a coarse grater.

3 Drain the carrot and add it to the grated potato with the celery, mushrooms, onion, peas and cheese. Season well.

4 Place all of the sauce ingredients in a pan and bring to the boil. Reduce the heat and simmer for 15 minutes.

5 Divide the potato mixture into 8 portions of equal size and shape into flattened rectangles with your hands.

6 Heat the oil and butter in a frying pan (skillet) and cook the hash browns over a low heat for 4-5 minutes on each side until crisp and golden brown.

7 Serve the hash browns with the tomato sauce.

COOK'S TIP

Use any mixture of vegetables for this recipe. For a non-vegetarian dish, add bacon pieces or diced ham for added flavour.

Spanish Tortilla

This classic Spanish dish is often served as part of a tapas *(appetizer) selection. A variety of cooked vegetables can be added to this recipe, making it an ideal way to use up leftovers.*

Serves 4

INGREDIENTS

1 kg/ 2.2 lb waxy potatoes, thinly
    sliced
4 tbsp vegetable oil
1 onion, sliced
2 garlic cloves, crushed

1 green (bell) pepper, diced
2 tomatoes, deseeded and
    chopped
25 g/1 oz canned sweetcorn,
    drained

6 large eggs, beaten
2 tbsp chopped fresh parsley
salt and pepper

1 Parboil the potatoes in a saucepan of boiling water for 5 minutes. Drain well.

2 Heat the oil in a large frying pan (skillet), add the potato and onions and sauté gently for 5 minutes, stirring constantly, until the potatoes have browned.

3 Add the garlic, diced (bell) pepper, chopped tomatoes and sweetcorn, mixing well.

4 Pour in the eggs and add the chopped parsley. Season well with salt and pepper. Cook for 10-12 minutes until the underside is cooked through.

5 Remove the frying pan (skillet) from the heat and continue to cook the tortilla under a preheated medium grill (broiler) for 5-7 minutes or until the tortilla is set and the top is golden brown.

6 Cut the tortilla into wedges or cubes, depending on your preference, and serve with salad. In Spain tortillas are served hot, cold or warm.

COOK'S TIP

Ensure that the handle of your pan is heatproof before placing it under the grill (broiler) and be sure to use an oven glove when removing it as it will be very hot.

Creamy Mushrooms & Potatoes

These oven-baked mushrooms are topped with a creamy potato and mushroom filling topped with melted cheese. Served with crisp green salad leaves they make a delicious light meal.

Serves 4

INGREDIENTS

25 g/1 oz dried ceps
225 g/8 oz floury (mealy) potatoes, diced
25 g/1 oz/2 tbsp butter, melted
4 tbsp double (heavy) cream

2 tbsp chopped fresh chives
25 g/1 oz Emmental cheese, grated
8 large open capped mushrooms
150 ml/^{1}/$_4$ pint/^{2}/$_3$ cup vegetable stock

salt and pepper
fresh chives, to garnish

1 Place the dried ceps in a bowl, cover with boiling water and leave to soak for 20 minutes.

2 Meanwhile, cook the potatoes in a saucepan of boiling water for 10 minutes until cooked. Drain well and mash.

3 Drain the soaked ceps and chop them finely. Mix them into the mashed potato.

4 Mix the butter, cream and chives together and pour into the cep and potato mixture. Season with salt and pepper.

5 Remove the stalks from the open-capped mushrooms. Chop the stalks and stir them into the potato mixture. Spoon the mixture into the open-capped mushrooms and sprinkle the cheese over the top.

6 Place the filled mushrooms in a shallow ovenproof dish and pour in the vegetable stock.

7 Cover the dish and cook in a preheated oven, 220°C/425°F/Gas Mark 7, for 20 minutes. Remove the lid and cook for 5 minutes until golden on top.

8 Garnish the mushrooms with fresh chives and serve at once.

VARIATION

Use fresh mushrooms instead of the dried ceps, if preferred, and stir a mixture of chopped nuts into the mushroom stuffing mixture for extra crunch.

Colcannon

This is an old Irish recipe, usually served with a piece of bacon,
but it is equally delicious with chicken or fish.

Serves 4

INGREDIENTS

225 g/8 oz green cabbage, shredded
85 ml/3 fl oz/^{1}/$_3$ cup milk
25 g/8 oz floury (mealy) potatoes,
  diced

1 large leek, chopped
pinch of grated nutmeg

15 g/^{1}/$_2$ oz/1 tbsp butter, melted
salt and pepper

1 Cook the shredded cabbage
in a saucepan of boiling salted
water for 7-10 minutes. Drain
thoroughly and set aside.

2 Meanwhile, in a separate
saucepan, bring the milk to
the boil and add the potatoes and
leek. Reduce the heat and simmer
for 15-20 minutes or until they are
cooked through.

3 Stir in the grated nutmeg and
mash the potatoes and leeks
together.

4 Add the drained cabbage to
the potatoes and mix well.

5 Spoon the potato and cabbage
mixture into a serving dish,
making a hollow in the centre with
the back of a spoon.

6 Pour the melted butter into
the hollow and serve the dish
immediately.

COOK'S TIP

There are many different varieties
of cabbage, which produce hearts
at varying times of year, so you
can be sure of being able to make
this delicious cabbage dish all
year round.

VARIATION

Add diced cooked bacon to the
recipe for extra flavour, adding it
with the leeks and cabbage.

Italian Potato Wedges

*These oven-cooked potato wedges use classic pizza ingredients and are
delicious served with plain meats, such as pork or lamb.*

Serves 4

INGREDIENTS

2 large waxy potatoes, unpeeled
4 large ripe tomatoes, peeled and
seeded
150 ml/¼ pint/²/₃ cup vegetable
stock

2 tbsp tomato purée (paste)
1 small yellow (bell) pepper, cut into
strips
125 g/4½ oz button mushrooms,
quartered

1 tbsp chopped fresh basil
50 g/1³/₄ oz cheese, grated
salt and pepper

1 Cut each of the potatoes into 8 equal wedges. Parboil the potatoes in a pan of boiling water for 15 minutes. Drain well and place in a shallow ovenproof dish.

2 Chop the tomatoes and add to the dish. Mix together the vegetable stock and tomato purée (paste), then pour the mixture over the potatoes and tomatoes.

3 Add the yellow (bell) pepper strips, quartered mushrooms and chopped basil. Season well with salt and pepper.

4 Sprinkle the grated cheese over the top and cook in a preheated oven, 190°C/375°F/Gas Mark 5, for 15-20 minutes until the topping is golden brown. Serve at once.

COOK'S TIP

For the topping, use any cheese that melts well, such as Mozzarella, the traditional pizza cheese. Alternatively, you could use either Gruyère or Emmental cheese, if you prefer.

COOK'S TIP

These potato wedges can also be served as a light supper dish, accompanied by chunks of crusty, fresh brown or white bread.

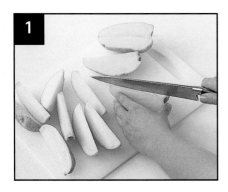

Chilli Roast Potatoes

A delicious variation of the traditional roast potato, here small new potatoes are scrubbed and boiled in their skins, before being coated in a chilli mixture and roasted to perfection in the oven.

Serves 4

INGREDIENTS

450 g/1 lb small new potatoes, scrubbed

150 ml/^{1}/$_4$ pint/^{2}/$_3$ cup vegetable oil

1 tsp chilli powder

^{1}/$_2$ tsp caraway seeds

1 tsp salt

1 tbsp chopped fresh basil

1 Cook the potatoes in a saucepan of boiling water for 10 minutes. Drain thoroughly.

2 Pour a little of the oil into a shallow roasting tin (pan) to coat the bottom of the tin (pan). Heat the oil in a preheated oven, 200°C/400°F/Gas Mark 6, for 10 minutes. Add the potatoes to the tin (pan) and brush them with the hot oil.

3 In a small bowl, mix together the chilli powder, caraway seeds and salt. Sprinkle the mixture over the potatoes, turning to coat them all over.

4 Add the remaining oil to the tin (pan) and roast in the oven for about 15 minutes or until the potatoes are cooked through.

5 Using a perforated spoon, remove the potatoes from the the oil, and transfer them to a warm serving dish. Sprinkle the chopped basil over the top and serve immediately.

VARIATION

Use any other spice of your choice, such as curry powder or paprika, for a variation in flavour.

COOK'S TIP

These spicy potatoes are ideal for serving with plain meat dishes, such as roasted or grilled lamb, pork or chicken.

Potatoes Dauphinois

This is a classic potato dish of layered potatoes, cream, garlic, onion and cheese.
Serve with poached fish, such as fresh salmon, or smoked fish for a delicious meal.

Serves 4

INGREDIENTS

15 g/^{1}/$_2$ oz/1 tbsp butter
675 g/1^1/$_2$ lb waxy potatoes, sliced
2 garlic cloves, crushed

1 red onion, sliced
75 g/3 oz Gruyère cheese, grated

300 ml/^{1}/$_2$ pint/1^1/$_4$ cups double
  (heavy) cream
salt and pepper

---

1 Lightly grease a 1 litre/1^3/$_4$ pint/4 cup shallow ovenproof dish with a little butter.

2 Arrange a single layer of potato slices in the base of the prepared dish.

3 Top the potato slices with a little of the garlic, sliced red onion and grated Gruyére cheese. Season to taste with a little salt and pepper.

4 Repeat the layers in exactly the same order, finishing with a layer of potatoes topped with cheese.

5 Pour the cream over the top of the potatoes and cook in a preheated oven, 180°C/350°F/Gas Mark 4, for 1^1/$_2$ hours or until the potatoes are cooked through, browned and crispy. Serve at once.

COOK'S TIP

There are many versions of this classic potato dish, but the different recipes always contain double (heavy) cream, making it a rich and very filling side dish or accompaniment. This recipe must be cooked in a shallow dish to ensure there is plenty of crispy topping.

VARIATION

Add a layer of chopped bacon or ham to this dish, if you prefer, and serve with a crisp green salad for a light supper.

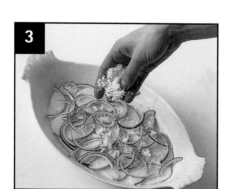

Casseroled Potatoes

This potato dish is cooked in the oven with leeks and wine.
It is very quick and simple to make.

Serves 4

INGREDIENTS

675 g/1$\frac{1}{2}$ lb waxy potatoes, cut into chunks
15 g/$\frac{1}{2}$ oz/1 tbsp butter
2 leeks, sliced
150 ml/$\frac{1}{4}$ pint/$\frac{2}{3}$ cup dry white wine

150 ml/$\frac{1}{4}$ pint/$\frac{2}{3}$ cup vegetable stock
1 tbsp lemon juice
2 tbsp chopped mixed fresh herbs
salt and pepper

TO GARNISH:
grated lemon rind
mixed fresh herbs (optional)

1 Cook the potato chunks in a saucepan of boiling water for 5 minutes. Drain thoroughly.

2 Meanwhile, melt the butter in a frying pan (skillet) and sauté the leeks for 5 minutes or until they have softened.

3 Spoon the partly cooked potatoes and leeks into the base of an ovenproof dish.

4 In a measuring jug, mix together the wine, vegetable stock, lemon juice and chopped mixed herbs. Season to taste with salt and pepper, then pour the mixture over the potatoes.

5 Cook in a preheated oven, 190°C/375°F/Gas Mark 5, for 35 minutes or until the potatoes are tender.

6 Garnish the potato casserole with lemon rind and fresh herbs, if using, and serve as an accompaniment to meat casseroles or roast meat.

COOK'S TIP

Cover the ovenproof dish halfway through cooking if the leeks start to brown on the top.

Cheese Crumble-Topped Mash

This is a delicious way to liven up mashed potato by topping it with a crumble mixture flavoured with herbs, mustard and onion, which turns crunchy on baking.

Serves 4

INGREDIENTS

900 g/2 lb floury (mealy) potatoes, diced
25 g/1 oz/2 tbsp butter
2 tbsp milk
50 g/1¾ oz mature (sharp) cheese or blue cheese, grated

CRUMBLE TOPPING:
40 g/1½ oz/3 tbsp butter
1 onion, cut into chunks
1 garlic clove, crushed
1 tbsp wholegrain mustard

175 g/ 6 oz/3 cups fresh wholemeal (whole wheat) breadcrumbs
2 tbsp chopped fresh parsley
salt and pepper

1 Cook the potatoes in a pan of boiling water for 10 minutes or until cooked through.

2 Meanwhile, make the crumble topping. Melt the butter in a frying pan (skillet). Add the onion, garlic and mustard and fry gently for 5 minutes until the onion chunks have softened, stirring constantly.

3 Put the breadcrumbs in a mixing bowl and stir in the fried onion. Season to taste with salt and pepper.

4 Drain the potatoes thoroughly and place them in a mixing bowl. Add the butter and milk, then mash until smooth. Stir in the grated cheese while the potato is still hot.

5 Spoon the mashed potato into a shallow ovenproof dish and sprinkle with the crumble topping.

6 Cook in a preheated oven, 200°C/400°F/Gas Mark 6, for 10-15 minutes until the crumble topping is golden brown and crunchy. Serve immediately.

COOK'S TIP

For extra crunch, add freshly cooked vegetables, such as celery and (bell) peppers, to the mashed potato in step 4.

Lamb Hotpot

No potato cookbook would be complete without this classic recipe using lamb cutlets layered between sliced potatoes, kidneys, onions and herbs.

Serves 4

INGREDIENTS

675 g/1¹/₂ lb best end of lamb neck cutlets
2 lamb's kidneys
675 g/1¹/₂ lb waxy potatoes, scrubbed and sliced thinly

1 large onion, sliced thinly
2 tbsp chopped fresh thyme
150 ml/¹/₄ pint/²/₃ cup lamb stock
25 g/1 oz/2 tbsp butter, melted

salt and pepper
fresh thyme sprigs, to garnish

1 Remove any excess fat from the lamb. Skin and core the kidneys and cut them into slices.

2 Arrange a layer of potatoes in the base of a 1.8 litre/3 pint/ 3¹/₂ cup ovenproof dish.

3 Arrange the lamb neck cutlets on top of the potatoes and cover with the sliced kidneys, onion and chopped fresh thyme.

4 Pour the lamb stock over the meat and season to taste with salt and pepper.

5 Layer the remaining potato slices on top, overlapping to completely cover the meat and sliced onion.

6 Brush the potato slices with the butter, cover the dish and cook in a preheated oven, 180°C/ 350°F/Gas Mark 4, for 1¹/₂ hours.

7 Remove the lid and cook for a further 30 minutes until golden brown on top.

8 Garnish with fresh thyme sprigs and serve hot.

COOK'S TIP

Although this is a classic recipe, extra ingredients of your choice, such as celery or carrots, can be added to the dish for variety and colour.

VARIATION

Traditionally, oysters are also included in this tasty hotpot. Add them to the layers along with the kidneys, if wished.

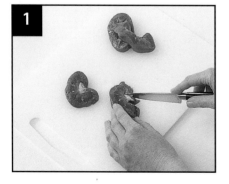

Spanish Potato Bake

This is a variation of a traditional Spanish dish, Huevos, where eggs are served on top of a tomato mixture. Here eggs are cooked on top of a spicy sausage, tomato and potato mixture.

Serves 4

INGREDIENTS

675 g/1¹/₂ lb waxy potatoes, diced
3 tbsp olive oil
1 onion, halved and sliced
2 garlic cloves, crushed
400 g/14 oz can plum tomatoes, chopped

75 g/2³/₄ oz chorizo sausage, sliced
1 green (bell) pepper, cut into strips
¹/₂ tsp paprika
25 g/1 oz stoned (pitted) black olives, halved
8 eggs

1 tbsp chopped fresh parsley
salt and pepper

1 Cook the diced potatoes in a saucepan of boiling water for 10 minutes or until softened. Drain and set aside.

2 Heat the olive oil in a large frying pan (skillet), add the sliced onion and garlic and fry gently for 2-3 minutes until the onion softens.

3 Add the chopped canned tomatoes and cook over a low heat for about 10 minutes until the mixture has reduced slightly.

4 Stir the potatoes into the pan with the chorizo, green (bell) pepper, paprika and olives. Cook for 5 minutes, stirring. Transfer to a shallow ovenproof dish.

5 Make 8 small hollows in the top of the mixture and break an egg into each hollow.

6 Cook in a preheated oven, 225°C/425°F/Gas Mark 7, for 5-6 minutes or until the eggs are just cooked. Sprinkle with parsley and serve with crusty bread.

VARIATION

Add a little spice to the dish by incorporating 1 tsp chilli powder in step 4, if wished.

Potato Curry

Very little meat is eaten in India, their diet being mainly vegetarian. This potato curry with added vegetables makes a very substantial main meal.

Serves 4

INGREDIENTS

4 tbsp vegetable oil
675 g/1 1/2 lb waxy potatoes, cut into large chunks
2 onions, quartered
3 garlic cloves, crushed
1 tsp garam masala
1/2 tsp turmeric

1/2 tsp ground cumin
1/2 tsp ground coriander
2.5 cm/1 inch piece ginger root, grated
1 red chilli, chopped
225 g/8 oz cauliflower florets
4 tomatoes, peeled and quartered

75 g/2 3/4 oz frozen peas
2 tbsp chopped fresh coriander (cilantro)
300 ml/1/2 pint/1 1/4 cups vegetable stock
shredded fresh coriander (cilantro), to garnish

1 Heat the vegetable oil in a large heavy-based saucepan or frying pan (skillet). Add the potato chunks, onion and garlic and fry gently for 2-3 minutes, stirring the mixture frequently.

2 Add the garam masala, turmeric, ground cumin, ground coriander, grated ginger and chopped chilli to the pan, mixing the spices into the vegetables. Fry for 1 minute, stirring constantly.

3 Add the cauliflower florets, tomatoes, peas, chopped coriander (cilantro) and vegetable stock to the curry mixture.

4 Cook the potato curry over a low heat for 30-40 minutes or until the potatoes are completely cooked through.

5 Garnish the potato curry with fresh coriander (cilantro) and serve with plain boiled rice or warm Indian bread.

COOK'S TIP

Use a large heavy-based saucepan or frying pan (skillet) for this recipe to ensure that the potatoes are cooked thoroughly.

Bubble & Squeak

Bubble and squeak is best known as mashed potato and leftover green vegetables cooked in meat fat in a pan and served as an accompaniment.

Serves 4

INGREDIENTS

450 g/1 lb floury (mealy) potatoes, diced
225 g/8 oz Savoy cabbage, shredded
5 tbsp vegetable oil

2 leeks, chopped
1 garlic clove, crushed
225 g/8 oz smoked tofu (bean curd), cubed

salt and pepper
shredded cooked leek, to garnish

1 Cook the diced potatoes in a saucepan of boiling water for 10 minutes until tender. Drain and mash the potatoes.

2 Meanwhile, in a separate saucepan blanch the cabbage in boiling water for 5 minutes. Drain and add to the potato.

3 Heat the oil in a heavy-based frying pan (skillet), add the leeks and garlic and fry gently for 2-3 minutes. Stir into the potato and cabbage mixture.

4 Add the smoked tofu (bean curd) and season well with salt and pepper. Cook over a moderate heat for 10 minutes.

5 Carefully turn the whole mixture over and continue to cook over a moderate heat for a further 5-7 minutes until crispy underneath. Serve immediately, garnished with shredded leek.

COOK'S TIP

This vegetarian recipe is a perfect main meal, as the smoked tofu (bean curd) cubes added to the basic bubble and squeak mixture make it very substantial.

VARIATION

You can add cooked meats, such as beef or chicken, instead of the tofu (bean curd) for a more traditional recipe. Any gravy from the cooked meats can also be added, but ensure that the mixture is not too wet.

Twice Baked Potatoes with Pesto

This is an easy but very filling meal. The potatoes are baked until fluffy, then the flesh is scooped out and mixed with a tasty pesto filling before being returned to the potato shells and baked again.

Serves 4

INGREDIENTS

4 baking potatoes, about 225 g/8 oz
  each
150 ml/^{1}/4 pint/^{2}/3 cup double
  (heavy) cream

85 ml/3 fl oz/^{1}/3 cup vegetable stock
1 tbsp lemon juice
2 garlic cloves, crushed
3 tbsp chopped fresh basil

2 tbsp pine kernels (nuts)
2 tbsp grated Parmesan cheese
salt and pepper

1 Scrub the potatoes and prick the skins with a fork. Rub a little salt into the skins and place on a baking (cookie) sheet.

2 Cook in a preheated oven, 190°C/375°F/Gas Mark 5, for 1 hour or until the potatoes are cooked through and the skins crisp.

3 Remove the potatoes from the oven and cut them in half lengthways. Using a spoon, scoop the potato flesh into a mixing bowl, leaving a thin shell of potato inside the skins. Mash the potato flesh with a fork.

4 Meanwhile, mix the cream and stock in a saucepan and simmer for 8-10 minutes or until reduced by half.

5 Stir in the lemon juice, garlic and chopped basil and season to taste with salt and pepper. Stir the mixture into the potato flesh with the pine kernels (nuts).

6 Spoon the mixture back into the potato shells and sprinkle the Parmesan cheese on top. Return the potatoes to the oven for 10 minutes or until the cheese has browned. Serve with salad.

VARIATION

Add full fat soft cheese or thinly sliced mushrooms to the mashed potato flesh in step 5, if you prefer.

Potato Crisp Pie

This is a layered pie of potatoes, broccoli, tomatoes and chicken slices in a creamy sauce, topped with a crisp oaty layer. Use strips of beef or pork for an equally delicious dish, if preferred.

Serves 4

INGREDIENTS

2 large waxy potatoes, sliced
60 g/2 oz/$^{1}/_4$ cup butter
1 skinned chicken breast fillet, about 175 g/6 oz
2 garlic cloves, crushed
4 spring onions (scallions), sliced

25 g/1 oz/$^{1}/_4$ cup plain (all-purpose) flour
150 ml/$^{1}/_4$ pint/$^{2}/_3$ cup dry white wine
150 ml/$^{1}/_4$ pint/$^{2}/_3$ cup double (heavy) cream

225 g/8 oz broccoli florets
4 large tomatoes, sliced
75 g/3 oz Gruyère cheese, sliced
225 ml/8 fl oz/1 cup natural yogurt
25 g/1 oz/$^{1}/_3$ cup rolled oats, toasted

1 Cook the potatoes in a saucepan of boiling water for 10 minutes. Drain and set aside.

2 Meanwhile, melt the butter in a frying pan (skillet). Cut the chicken into strips and cook for 5 minutes, turning. Add the garlic and spring onions (scallions) and cook for a further 2 minutes.

3 Stir in the flour and cook for 1 minute. Gradually add the wine and cream. Bring to the boil, stirring, then reduce the heat until the sauce is simmering, then cook for 5 minutes.

4 Meanwhile, blanch the broccoli in boiling water, drain and refresh in cold water.

5 Place half of the potatoes in the base of a pie dish and top with half of the tomatoes and half of the broccoli.

6 Spoon the chicken sauce on top and repeat the layers in the same order once more.

7 Arrange the Gruyère cheese on top and spoon over the yogurt. Sprinkle with the oats and cook in a preheated oven, 200°C/400°F/Gas Mark 6, for 25 minutes until the top is golden brown. Serve the pie immediately.

COOK'S TIP

Add chopped nuts, such as pine kernels (nuts), to the topping for extra crunch, if you prefer.

Layered Fish & Potato Pie

This is a really delicious and filling dish. Layers of potato slices and mixed fish are cooked in a creamy sauce and topped with grated cheese.

Serves 4

INGREDIENTS

900 g/2 lb waxy potatoes, sliced
60 g/2 oz/¼ cup butter
1 red onion, halved and sliced
50 g/1¾ oz/⅓ cup plain (all-purpose) flour

450 ml/¾ pint/2 cups milk
150 ml/¼ pint double (heavy) cream
225 g/8 oz smoked haddock fillet, cubed
225 g/8 oz cod fillet, cubed

1 red (bell) pepper, diced
125 g/4½ oz broccoli florets
50 g/1¾ oz Parmesan cheese, grated
salt and pepper

1 Cook the sliced potatoes in a saucepan of boiling water for 10 minutes. Drain and set aside.

2 Meanwhile, melt the butter in a saucepan, add the onion and fry gently for 3-4 minutes.

3 Add the flour and cook for 1 minute. Blend in the milk and cream and bring to the boil, stirring until the sauce has thickened.

4 Arrange half of the potato slices in the base of a shallow ovenproof dish.

5 Add the fish, diced (bell) pepper and broccoli to the sauce and cook over a low heat for 10 minutes. Season with salt and pepper, then spoon the mixture over the potatoes in the dish.

6 Arrange the remaining potato slices in a layer over the fish mixture. Sprinkle the Parmesan cheese over the top.

7 Cook in a preheated oven, 180°C/350°F/Gas Mark 4, for 30 minutes or until the potatoes are cooked and the top is golden.

COOK'S TIP

Choose your favourite combination of fish, adding salmon or various shellfish for special occasions.

This is a Parragon Book
First published in 2003

Parragon
Queen Street House
4 Queen Street, Bath, BA1 1HE, UK

Copyright © Parragon 2003

All recipes and photography compiled from material cre-
ated by 'Haldane Mason', and 'The Foundry'.

Cover design by Shelley Doyle.

ISBN: 1-40540-830-8

Printed in China

NOTE

This book uses imperial and metric measurements. Follow the same
units of measurement throughout; do not mix imperial and metric. All
spoon measurements are level; teaspoons are assumed to be 5 ml and
tablespoons are assumed to be 15 ml. Unless otherwise stated, milk is
assumed to be whole milk, eggs and individual vegetables such as potatoes are medium, and pepper is freshly ground black pepper.

The times given for each recipe are an approximate guide only because
the preparation times may differ according to the techniques used by different people and the cooking times may vary as a result of the type of
oven used.

Recipes using raw or very lightly cooked eggs should be avoided by
infants, the elderly, pregnant women, convalescents and anyone suffer-
ing from an illness.